Sweet and Cheeky Nicknames for Your Baby

ISBN: 0-9764145-03

Printed in the United States of America

To all my one-time
itty bittees, Chris, Grant, Nick,
Myles, Maxx, and Dante.
And to Beth Ann who fills
our home with fun and love.
~
RJM

To Norman Samuel Walker,
my Little Peanut
~
SMW

Little Tiger

Little Tiger

(aka. Smallus Growlus)

This baby is known to be swift,
playful, and adventurous.
Responds well to tickles, hugs
and general roughhousing.
On rare occasions has been
known to turn on its handlers.
Experts advise lots of activity,
food, and a strong playpen.

~

Chunky Monkey

Chunky Monkey

(aka. Pudgus Activus)

Sometimes mistaken for having rubberbands on its wrists and legs, this creature draws pinches and coos from strangers and relatives. Known to be one of the cutest species of babies who never turns down a good meal. If not kept busy, this baby can also get into plenty of mischief and then charm parents with a simple smile.

~

Creepy Crawler

Creepy Crawler

(aka. Stealthus Movus)

While other babies are busy trying to roll over or sit up, Creepy Crawlers move deliberately at their own pace. It is not uncommon for them to crawl back and forth for hours at a time. They respond well to shiny objects and parents who beckon from a few feet away.

~

Party Girl

Party Girl
(aka. Girlus Celebratorium)

This fun creature likes clothes, noise and plenty of people to entertain. Often found in the middle of the action, the Party Girl likes to babble and is very social. When partygoers are not available, she is known to press her favorite stuffed animals into service. Though generally happy, experts warn that the end of a party can bring on tantrums and general defiance.

~

Princess

Princess

(aka. Girlus Royalus)

Once the princess comes home,
it is clear who is the boss. Whether
charming her subjects with smiles
or prodding them with loud
utterances, she manages to get
what she needs and wants.
But this reciprocal relationship
flourishes because it gives parents
and grandparents a chance to serve
and gives the Princess a chance
to be adored.

~

Pumpkin

Pumpkin

(aka. Gourdus Orangus)

These cuddly little packages feel surprisingly solid in your arms. Though not as pudgy as a Chunky Monkey, there is a pleasing roundness to their overall shape. In general, Pumpkins are good-natured and nearly as agreeable as Sweet Peas. Parents report that there are better chances for siblings if their first child is a Pumpkin.

~

Little Monkey

Little Monkey

(aka. Activus Climbus)

A close relative of the Chunky Monkey, these babies are agile, quick, and daring. Reports of Little Monkeys climbing out of bassinets, highchairs, and car seats are not uncommon. Legend has it that one especially nimble baby even climbed to the top of a dresser! Experts and bystanders recommend plenty of exercise and a GPS tracking device to monitor their movements.

~

Boo Boo

Boo Boo

(aka. Exclamator Surprisi)

This baby is known to be wide-eyed, quiet, and agreeable. Ever curious, a Boo Boo steadily moves around a room and examines objects with their eyes, hands, and mouth. Having an understated cuteness about them, adults are drawn to their gentle confidence and look of perpetual interest. At times, when fully engaged and on the move, they can be mistaken for a "Little Ham".

~

Love Bug

Love Bug

(aka. Amor Insecti)

Caregivers report strong feelings of attachment when introduced to the Love Bug. This little one likes to cuddle, coo and take naps in people's arms. The Love Bug is also one of the few babies who will willingly wear cute hats and clothes. In addition, the Love Bug is an excellent traveler and welcome on all forms of public transportation.

~

Little Peanut

Little Peanut

(aka. Legume Popular)

Even at birth, the Little Peanut is smaller and some would say cuter than its peers. Able to stay in the same clothing size for an extended period of time, this little one is probably the best dressed baby on the block. Inexperienced parents will be surprised at the amount of food a Little Peanut can consume and it is anyone's guess whether he or she will remain small or grow taller than once bigger peers.

~

Milk Monster

Milk Monster

(aka. Leche Grande Consumorous)

If this infant could talk they would adamantly say things such as, “Get in my belly!” “Feed me!” or “I want more milk!” When full, the Milk Monster calms down and often sleeps for long periods. Beware, however, that upon waking the feeding cycle soon begins. Smart parents have been known to set aside additional funds to pay for food through the teenage years when consumption patterns can be absolutely frightening!

~

Binky Boy & Binky Girl

Binky Boy & Binky Girl

(aka. Better Than Thumbus)

When the thumb is not enough, the Binky Boy and Binky Girl require their binky, pacy, pucky, nuk, tati or any number of code words that mean one thing – "get-me-my-pacifier-and-get-it-fast!" At times, they can actually talk, color, play and eat calmly while the "Almighty" pacifier is in the mouth. Any parent will tell you, this is one habit you have to face with patience, support, and resolve – but eventually this, too, will pass.

~

Spitting Image

Spitting Image
(aka. Samus DNAus)

Sometimes one parent's genes are so dominant that the offspring look like a mini version of the parent. From subtle facial features like the way an eyebrow curves to more noticeable features like the shape of a chin, this little one is a much younger version of the parent. At times, Moms and Dads have been known to dress in the same outfit as their child to great comic effect or a wonderful show of solidarity and fun.

~

Little Ham

Little Ham

(aka. Tini Actori)

If top hats and tiaras were available in baby sizes, this little one would surely be wearing one or the other. With a little patience and practice, tricks such as high fives, one-eyed winks, and looks of surprise can become part of the Little Ham's repertoire. This baby is also known to have a high quotient of charisma or "it." Other traits of the Little Ham include a healthy appetite and sound sleep cycle.

~

Little Snuggler

Little Snuggler

(aka. Likes to Huggus)

Similar to the Little Bear, the Little Snuggler is exactly what it's name implies. Affectionate, cuddly, and always seemingly warm, this baby loves to be held and snuggled. When rocked, this baby is especially happy. When held they also enjoy looking at picture books, receiving gentle tickles, and light roughhousing. Experts add that even after a bad day, the Little Snuggler can make any beleaguered parent feel better.

~

Little Mouse

Little Mouse

(aka. Quiete Squeakus)

Found in many peaceful homes, the Little Mouse quietly goes about its business of sleeping, eating and playing. Even at a tender age the Little Mouse seems to value peace and quiet. Sporting a modest appetite and gentle demeanor, this one is equally as happy being the center of attention or spending time alone. On occasion can be fussy but even then is easily pleased.

~

Little Bear

Little Bear

(aka. Ursulasus Minor)

Cuddly, warm and sweet, a Little Bear likes to sleep in mom and dad's bed and prefers to be held at all times. Much like a stuffed animal, they are soft and have that indescribable unique scent. When not hibernating, they prefer a good meal and lots of attention. As a sibling, a Little Bear is supportive, sweet and patient. Parents who have a Little Bear are truly blessed.

~

Sweet Pea

Sweet Pea

(aka. Good Naturus Infantus)

Parents who are blessed with
a Sweat Pea are enviable.
They wake up happy, eat well at
predictable times, sleep through
the night, and rarely cry.
A Sweat Pea is also known to be
pleasant to strangers and freely
share their toothless grin. Though
most people believe they are
mythical beings, just last year a
Sweat Pea was reported seen in
Poughkeepsie, NY.

~

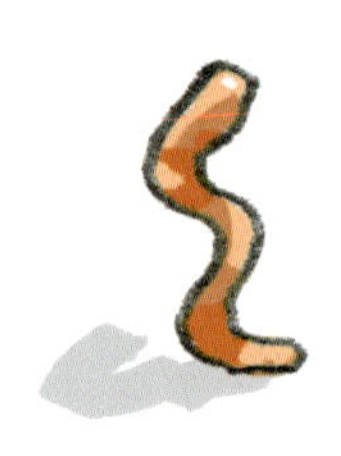

Wiggle Worm

Wiggle Worm

(aka. Undulus Squirmius)

Especially active when confronted with a new diaper, this little one can move like a wrestler. Upon capture, movement will continue on any part of the body that is not secured. Experienced parents recommend lots of daily activity. If possible, a Wiggle Worm should be handled by a minimum of two adults.

~

Little Stinker

Little Stinker

(aka. Smellus to High Heavenus)

If you smell an odor that
is not common in nature, you most
likely have a Little Stinker on
your hands. An iron will, a Diaper
Genie, and swift calculated actions
will allow you to survive the early
years of this little one. If possible,
experts recommend parents
take turns when changing
the Little Stinker.

~